# Windows 10:

# The Ultimate Beginner's Guide

## Lee Maxwell

## © 2016

# TABLE OF CONTENT

# Introduction

I want to thank you and congratulate you for downloading the book, *"Windows 10: The Ultimate Beginner's Guide"*.

This book contains proven steps and strategies on how to handle WINDOW 10... **Windows 10 is a personal computer** Operating system developed and released by Microsoft as part of the Windows NT family of operating systems. It was officially unveiled in September 2014 following a brief demo at Build 2014. The first version of the operating system entered a public beta testing process in October, leading up to its consumer release on July 29, 2015.

Windows 10 introduces what Microsoft described as "universal apps"; expanding on Metro-style apps, these apps can be designed to run across multiple Microsoft product families with nearly identical code—including PCs, tablets, smartphones, embedded systems, Xbox One, Surface Hub and Windows Holographic. The Windows user interface was revised to handle transitions between a mouse-oriented interface and a touchscreen-optimized interface based on available input devices—particularly on 2-in-1 PCs; both interfaces include an updated Start menu which incorporates elements of Windows 7's traditional Start menu with the tiles of Windows 8. The first release of Windows 10 also introduces a virtual desktop system, a window and desktop management feature called Task View, the Microsoft Edge web browser, support for fingerprint and face recognition login, new security features for enterprise environments, and DirectX 12 and WDDM 2.0 to improve the operating system's graphics capabilities for games.

Microsoft described Windows 10 as an "operating system as a service" that would receive ongoing updates to its features and functionality, augmented with the ability for enterprise environments to receive non-critical updates at a slower pace, or use long-term support milestones that will only receive critical updates, such as security patches, over their five-year lifespan of mainstream support. Terry Myerson, executive vice president of Microsoft's Windows and Devices Group, argued that the goal of this model was to reduce fragmentation across the Windows platform, as Microsoft aimed to have Windows 10 installed on at least one billion devices in the two to three years following its release.

Windows 10 received mostly positive reviews upon its original release in July 2015; critics praised Microsoft's decision to downplay user-interface mechanics introduced by Windows 8 (including the full screen apps and Start screen) in non-touch environments to provide a desktop-oriented interface in line with previous versions of Windows, although Windows 10's touch-oriented user interface mode was panned for containing regressions upon the touch-oriented interface of Windows 8. Critics also praised the improvements to Windows 10's bundled software over Windows 8.1, Xbox Live integration, as well as the functionality and capabilities of Cortana personal assistant and the replacement of Internet Explorer with Microsoft Edge.

Thanks again for downloading this book, I hope you enjoy it!

# Chapter 1

## Windows 10 is a personal computer

Operating system developed and released by Microsoft as part of the Windows NT family of operating systems. It was officially unveiled in September 2014 following a brief demo at Build 2014. The first version of the operating system entered a public beta testing process in October, leading up to its consumer release on July 29, 2015.

Windows 10 introduces what Microsoft described as "universal apps"; expanding on Metro-style apps, these apps can be designed to run across multiple Microsoft product families with nearly identical code—including PCs, tablets, smartphones, embedded systems, Xbox One, Surface Hub and Windows Holographic. The Windows user interface was revised to handle transitions between a mouse-oriented interface and a touchscreen-optimized interface based on available input devices—particularly on 2-in-1 PCs; both interfaces include an updated Start menu which incorporates elements of Windows 7's traditional Start menu with the tiles of Windows 8. The first release of Windows 10 also introduces a virtual desktop system, a window and desktop management feature called Task View, the Microsoft Edge web browser, support for fingerprint and face recognition login, new security features for enterprise environments, and DirectX 12 and WDDM 2.0 to improve the operating system's graphics capabilities for games.

Microsoft described Windows 10 as an "operating system as a service" that would receive ongoing updates to its features and functionality, augmented with the ability for enterprise environments to receive non-critical updates at a slower pace, or use long-term support milestones that will only receive critical updates, such as security patches, over their five-year lifespan of mainstream support. Terry Myerson, executive vice president of Microsoft's Windows and Devices Group, argued that the goal of this model was to reduce fragmentation across the Windows platform, as Microsoft aimed to have Windows 10 installed on at least one billion devices in the two to three years following its release.

Windows 10 received mostly positive reviews upon its original release in July 2015; critics praised Microsoft's decision to downplay user-interface mechanics introduced by Windows 8 (including the full screen apps and Start screen) in non-touch environments to provide a desktop-oriented interface in line with previous versions of Windows, although Windows 10's touch-oriented user interface mode was panned for containing regressions upon the touch-oriented interface of Windows 8. Critics also praised the improvements to Windows 10's bundled software over Windows 8.1, Xbox Live integration, as well as the functionality and capabilities of Cortana personal assistant and the replacement of Internet Explorer with Microsoft Edge.

Critics characterized the initial release of Windows 10 in July 2015 as being rushed, citing the incomplete state of some of the operating system's bundled software (such as the Edge web browser), as well as the stability of the operating system itself on launch. Windows 10 was also criticized for limiting how users can control its operation, including limited controls over the installation of updates on the main consumer-oriented edition in comparison to previous versions. Privacy concerns were also voiced by critics and advocates, as the operating system's default settings and certain features require the transmission of user data to Microsoft or its partners. Microsoft has also received criticism for how it has distributed Windows 10 to users of existing versions of Windows, which has included the automatic downloads of installation files to computers, the recurring display of pop-ups advertising the upgrade, and allegations of the installation process being scheduled or initiated automatically without expressed user consent.

Up to August 2016, Windows 10 usage was increasing, with it then plateauing, and with previous versions of Windows declining in their share of total usage as measured by web traffic. The operating system is running on more than 400 million active devices and has an estimated usage share of 24.43%; on traditional PCs and 12.08% across all platforms (PC, mobile, tablet, and console).

Development

At the Microsoft Worldwide Partner Conference in 2011, Andrew Lees, the chief of Microsoft's mobile technologies, said that the company intended to have a single software ecosystem for PCs, phones, tablets, and other devices. "We won't have an ecosystem for PCs, and one for phones, and one for tablets—they'll all come together."

In December 2013, technology writer Mary Jo Foley reported that Microsoft was working on an update to Windows 8 codenamed "Threshold", after a planet in Microsoft's Halo video game franchise. Similarly to "Blue" (which became Windows 8.1), Foley called Threshold a "wave of operating systems" across multiple Microsoft platforms and services, scheduled for the second quarter of 2015. Foley reported that among the goals for Threshold was to create a unified application platform and development toolkit for Windows, Windows Phone and Xbox One (which all use a similar Windows NT kernel).

In April 2014, at the Build Conference, Microsoft's Terry Myerson unveiled an updated version of Windows 8.1 that added the ability to run Windows Store apps inside desktop windows and a more traditional Start menu in place of the Start screen seen in Windows 8. The new Start menu takes after Windows 7's design by using only a portion of the screen and including a Windows 7-style application listing in the first column. The second column displays Windows 8-style app tiles. Myerson said that these changes would occur in a future update, but did not elaborate. Microsoft also unveiled the concept of a "universal Windows app", allowing Windows Store apps created for Windows 8.1 to be ported to Windows Phone 8.1 and Xbox One while sharing a common codebase, with an interface designed for different device form factors, and allowing user data and licenses for an app to be shared between multiple platforms. Windows Phone 8.1 would share nearly 90% of the common Windows Runtime APIs with Windows 8.1 on PCs.

Screenshots of a Windows build which purported to be Threshold were leaked in July 2014, showing the previously presented Start menu and windowed Windows Store apps followed by a further screenshot in September 2014 of a build identifying itself as "Windows Technical Preview", numbered 9834, showing a new virtual desktop system, a notification center, and a new File Explorer icon.

Announcement

Threshold was officially unveiled during a media event on September 30, 2014, under the name Windows 10; Myerson said that Windows 10 would be Microsoft's "most comprehensive platform ever", providing a single, unified platform for desktop computers, laptops, tablets, smartphones, and all-in-one devices. He emphasized that Windows 10 would take steps towards restoring user interface mechanics from Windows 7 to improve the experience for users on non-touch devices, noting criticism of Windows 8's touch-oriented interface by keyboard and mouse users. Despite these concessions, Myerson noted that the touch-oriented interface would evolve as well on 10.[38] In describing the changes, Joe Belfiore likened the two operating systems to electric cars, comparing Windows 7 to a first-generation Toyota Prius hybrid, and Windows 10 to an all-electric Tesla—considering the latter to be an extension of the technology first introduced in the former.

In regards to Microsoft naming the new operating system Windows 10 instead of Windows 9, Terry Myerson said that "based on the product that's coming, and just how different our approach will be overall, it wouldn't be right to call it Windows 9." He also joked that they could not call it "Windows One" (alluding to several recent Microsoft products with a similar brand, such as OneDrive, OneNote, and Xbox One) because Windows 1.0 already existed. Tony Prophet, Microsoft Vice President of Windows Marketing, said at a San Francisco conference in October 2014 that Windows 9 "came and went", and that Windows 10 is not "an incremental step from Windows 8.1," but "a material step. We're trying to create one platform, one eco-system that unites as many of the devices [sic] from the small embedded Internet of Things, through tablets, through phones, through PCs and, ultimately, into the Xbox."

Further details surrounding Windows 10's consumer-oriented features were presented during another media event held on January 21, 2015, entitled "Windows 10: The Next Chapter". The keynote featured the unveiling of Cortana integration within the operating system, new Xbox-oriented features, Windows 10 Mobile, an updated Office Mobile suite, Surface Hub—a large-screened Windows 10 device for enterprise collaboration based upon Perceptive Pixel technology, along with HoloLens-augmented reality eyewear and an associated platform for building apps that can render holograms through HoloLens.

Additional developer-oriented details surrounding the "Universal Windows Platform" concept were revealed and discussed during Microsoft's developers' conference Build. Among them were the unveiling of "Islandwood", which provides a middleware toolchain for compiling Objective-C based software (particularly, iOS software) to run as universal apps on Windows 10 and Windows 10 Mobile. A port of Candy Crush Saga made using the toolkit, which shared much of its code with the iOS version, was demonstrated, alongside the announcement that the King-developed game would be bundled with Windows 10 at launch.

Release

On June 1, 2015, Microsoft announced that Windows 10 would be released on July 29, 2015. Microsoft began an advertising campaign centering on Windows 10, "Upgrade Your World", on

July 20, 2015 with the premiere of television commercials in Australia, Canada, France, Germany, Japan, the United Kingdom, and the United States. The commercials focused on the tagline "A more human way to do", emphasizing new features and technologies supported by Windows 10 that sought to provide a more "personal" experience to users. The campaign culminated with launch events in thirteen cities on July 29, which celebrated "the unprecedented role our biggest fans played in the development of Windows 10".

# Chapter 2

Features

Features new to Windows 10

Windows 10 harmonizes the user experience and functionality between different classes of device, and addresses shortcomings in the user interface that were introduced in Windows 8. Windows 10 Mobile, the successor to Windows Phone 8.1, shares some user interface elements and apps with its PC counterpart.

The Windows Runtime app ecosystem was revised into the Universal Windows Platform (UWP). These universal apps are made to run across multiple platforms and device classes, including smartphones, tablets, Xbox One consoles, and other compatible Windows 10 devices. Windows apps share code across platforms, have responsive designs that adapt to the needs of the device and available inputs, can synchronize data between Windows 10 devices (including notifications, credentials, and allowing cross-platform multiplayer for games), and are distributed through a unified Windows Store. Developers can allow "cross-buys", where purchased licenses for an app apply to all of the user's compatible devices, rather than only the one they purchased on (e.g., a user purchasing an app on PC is also entitled to use the smartphone version at no extra cost).

On Windows 10, Windows Store serves as a unified storefront for apps, Groove Music (formerly Xbox Music), and Movies & TV (formerly Xbox Video). Windows 10 also allows web apps and desktop software (using either Win32 or .NET Framework) to be packaged for distribution on the Windows Store. Desktop software distributed through Windows Store is packaged using the App-V system to allow sandboxing.

User interface and desktop

A new iteration of the Start menu is used on the Windows 10 desktop, with a list of places and other options on the left side, and tiles representing applications on the right. The menu can be resized, and expanded into a full-screen display, which is the default option in Tablet mode. A new virtual desktop system was added. A feature known as Task View displays all open windows and allows users to switch between them, or switch between multiple workspaces. Windows Store apps, which previously could be used only in full screen mode, can now be used in self-contained windows similarly to other programs. Program windows can now be snapped to *q*uadrants of the screen by dragging them to the corner. When a window is snapped to one side of the screen, Task View appears and the user is prompted to choose a second window to fill the unused side of the screen (called "Snap Assist"). Windows' system icons were also changed.

Charms have been removed; their functionality in Windows Store apps is accessed from an App commands menu on their title bar. In its place is Action

Center, which displays notifications and settings toggles. It is accessed by clicking an icon in the notification area, or dragging from the right of the screen. Notifications can be synced between multiple devices. The Settings app (formerly PC Settings) was refreshed and now includes more options that were previously exclusive to the desktop Control Panel.

Windows 10 is designed to adapt its user interface based on the type of device being used and available input methods. It offers two separate user interface modes: a user interface optimized for mouse and keyboard, and a "Tablet mode" designed for touchscreens. Users can toggle between these two modes at any time, and Windows can prompt or automatically switch when certain events occur, such as disabling Tablet mode on a tablet if a keyboard or mouse is plugged in, or when a 2-in-1 PC is switched to its laptop state. In Tablet mode, programs default to a maximized view, and the taskbar contains a back button and hides buttons for opened or pinned programs; Task View is used instead to switch between programs. The full screen Start menu is used in this mode, similarly to Windows 8, but scrolls vertically instead of horizontally.

System security

Windows 10 incorporates multi-factor authentication technology based upon standards developed by the FIDO Alliance.[67] The operating system includes improved support for biometric authentication through the Windows Hello and Passport platforms; devices with supported cameras (requiring infrared illumination, such as Intel RealSense) allow users to log in with iris or face recognition, similarly to Kinect. Devices with supported readers support fingerprint-recognition login. Credentials are stored locally and protected using asymmetric encryption. The Passport platform allows networks, software and websites to authenticate users using either a PIN or biometric login to verify their identity, without sending a password.

The enterprise version of Windows 10 offers additional security features; administrators can set up policies for the automatic encryption of sensitive data, selectively block applications from accessing encrypted data, and enable Device Guard—a system which allows administrators to enforce a high security environment by blocking the execution of software that is not digitally signed by a trusted vendor or Microsoft. Device Guard is designed to protect against zero-day exploits, and runs inside a hypervisor so that its operation remains separated from the operating system itself.

Command line

Win32 console windows can now be resized without any restrictions, can be made to cover the full screen by pressing Alt+↵ Enter, and can use standard keyboard shortcuts, such as those for cut, copy, and paste. Other features such as word wrap and transparency were also added. These functions can be disabled to revert to the legacy console, if needed.

 Windows 10 version 1607 ("Redstone") adds Windows Subsystem for Linux, a version of the Ubuntu user space that can run natively on Windows. The subsystem translates Linux system calls that Ubuntu uses to those of the Windows NT kernel. This allows the Bash and other 64-bit Ubuntu command line apps to run within the Windows console; however, Bash cannot run Windows software and Windows cannot run Linux software.

Storage requirements

To reduce the storage footprint of the operating system, Windows 10 automatically compresses system files. The system can reduce the storage footprint of Windows by approximately 1.5 GB for 32-bit systems and 2.6 GB for 64-bit systems. The level of compression used is dependent on a performance assessment performed during installations or by OEMs, which tests how much compression can be used without harming operating system performance. Furthermore, the Refresh and Reset functions use runtime system files instead, making a separate recovery partition redundant, allowing patches and updates to remain installed following the operation, and further reducing the amount of space required for Windows 10 by up to 12 GB. These functions replace the WIMBoot mode introduced on Windows 8.1 Update, which allowed OEMs to configure low-capacity devices with flash-based storage to use Windows system files out of the compressed WIM image typically used for installation and recovery. Windows 10 also includes a function in its Settings app that allows users to view a breakdown of how their device's storage capacity is being used by different types of files, and determine whether certain types of files are saved to internal storage or an SD card by default.

Online services and functionality

Windows 10 introduces a new default web browser, Microsoft Edge. It features a new standards-compliant rendering engine forked from Trident, annotation tools, and offers integration with other Microsoft platforms present within Windows 10. Internet Explorer 11 is maintained on Windows 10 for compatibility purposes, but is deprecated in favor of Edge and will no longer be actively developed.

Windows 10 incorporates Microsoft's intelligent personal assistant, Cortana, which was first introduced with Windows Phone 8.1 in 2014. Cortana replaced Windows' embedded search feature, supporting both text and voice input. Many of its features are a direct carryover from Windows Phone, including integration with Bing, setting reminders, a Notebook feature for managing personal information, as well as searching for files, playing music, launching applications and setting reminders or sending emails.[85][86] Cortana is implemented as a universal search box located alongside the Start and Task View buttons, which can be hidden or condensed to a single button.

Microsoft Family Safety is replaced by Microsoft Family, a parental controls system that applies across Windows platforms and Microsoft online services. Users can create a designated family, and monitor and restrict the actions of users designated as children, such as access to websites, enforcing age ratings on Windows Store purchases, and other restrictions. The service can also send weekly e-mail reports to parents detailing a child's computer usage. Unlike previous versions of Windows, Child accounts in a family must be associated with a Microsoft account—which allows these settings to apply across all Windows 10 devices that a particular child is using.

Windows 10 also offers the Wi-Fi Sense feature originating from Windows Phone 8.1; users can optionally have their device automatically connect to suggested open hotspots, and share their home network's password with contacts (either via Skype, People, or Facebook) so they may automatically connect to the network on a Windows 10 device without needing to manually enter its password. Credentials are stored in an encrypted form on Microsoft servers, and sent to the devices of the selected contacts. Passwords are not viewable by the guest user, and the guest user is not allowed to access other computers or devices on the network. Wi-Fi Sense is not usable on 802.1X-encrypted networks. Adding "_optout" at the end of the SSID will also block the corresponding network from being used for this feature.


Universal calling and messaging apps for Windows 10 are built in as of the November 2015 update: Messaging, Skype Video, and Phone. These offer built-in alternatives to the Skype download and sync with Windows 10 Mobile.

# Chapter 3

## Multimedia and gaming

Windows 10 provides heavier integration with the Xbox ecosystem. Xbox SmartGlass is succeeded by the Xbox App, which allows users to browse their game library (including both PC and Xbox console games), and Game DVR is also available using a keyboard shortcut, allowing users to save the last 30 seconds of gameplay as a video that can be shared to Xbox Live, OneDrive, or elsewhere. Windows 10 also allows users to control and play games from an Xbox One console over a local network. The Xbox Live SDK allows application developers to incorporate Xbox Live functionality into their apps, and future wireless Xbox One accessories, such as controllers, are supported on Windows with an adapter. Microsoft also intends to allow cross-buys and save synchronization between Xbox One and Windows 10 versions of games; Microsoft Studios games such as ReCore and Quantum Break are intended as being exclusive to Windows 10 and Xbox One.

Candy Crush Saga and Microsoft Solitaire Collection are also automatically installed upon installation of Windows 10.

Windows 10 adds native game recording and screenshot capture ability using the newly introduced game bar. Users can also have the OS continuously record gameplay in the background, which, then, allows the user to save the last few, user configurable, moments of gameplay to the hard disk.

Windows 10 adds FLAC and HEVC codecs and support for the Matroska media container, allowing these formats to be opened in Windows Media Player and other applications.

DirectX 12

Windows 10 includes DirectX 12, alongside WDDM 2.0. Unveiled March 2014 at GDC, DirectX 12 aims to provide "console-level efficiency" with "closer to the metal" access to hardware resources, and reduced CPU and graphics driver overhead.[105][106] Most of the performance improvements are achieved through low-level programming, which allow developers to use resources more efficiently and reduce single-threaded CPU bottlenecking caused by abstraction through higher level APIs. DirectX 12 will also feature support for vendor agnostic multi-GPU setups.[109] WDDM 2.0 introduces a new virtual memory management and allocation system to reduce workload on the kernel-mode driver.

Removed features

Windows Media Center was discontinued, and is uninstalled when upgrading from a previous version of Windows. Upgraded Windows installations with Media Center will receive the paid app Windows DVD Player free of charge for a limited, but unspecified, time. Microsoft had previously relegated Media Center and integrated DVD playback support to a paid add-on beginning on Windows 8 due to the cost of licensing the required DVD decoders, and the increasing number of PC devices that have no optical drives.

The OneDrive built-in sync client, which was introduced in Windows 8.1, no longer supports offline placeholders for online-only files in Windows 10.Functionality to view offline files is expected to be added in the future by a new Windows app.

Users are no longer able to synchronize Start menu layouts across all devices associated with a Microsoft account. A Microsoft developer justified the change by explaining that a user may have different applications they want to emphasize on each device that they use, rather than use the same configuration across each device. The ability to automatically install a Windows Store app across all devices associated with an account was also removed.

Web browsers can no longer set themselves as a user's default without further intervention; changing the default web browser must be performed manually by the user from Settings' "Default apps" page, ostensibly to prevent browser hijacking.

Parental controls no longer support browsers other than Internet Explorer and Edge, and the ability to control browsing by a whitelist was removed. Also removed were the ability to control local accounts, and the ability to scan a machine for applications to allow and block.

The Food & Drink, Health & Fitness, and Travel apps have been discontinued.

Drivers for floppy drives are no longer integrated and must be downloaded separately.

While all Windows 10 editions include fonts that provide broad language support, some fonts for Middle Eastern and East Asian languages (Arabic, Chinese, Hindi, Japanese, Korean, etc.) are no longer included with the standard installation to reduce storage space used, but are available without charge as optional font packages. When software invokes text in languages other than those for which the system is configured and does not use the Windows font fallback mechanisms designed always to display legible glyphs, Windows displays unsupported characters as a default "not defined" glyph, a s*q*uare or rectangular box, or a box with a dot, *q*uestion mark or "x" inside.

Windows Defender could be integrated into File Explorer's context menu in Windows 8.x, but Microsoft initially removed integration from Windows 10, restoring it in Windows 10 build 10571 in response to user feedback.

User control over Windows Updates was removed (except in enterprise versions). In earlier versions users could opt for updates to be installed automatically, or to be notified so they could update as and when they wished, or not to be notified; and they could choose which updates to install, using information about the updates. Windows 10 Pro and Enterprise users may be configured by an administrator to defer updates, but only for a limited time. For example, in its Canadian licensing agreement, users of Windows 10 "may stop receiving updates on your device by turning off Internet access. If and when you re-connect to the Internet, the software will resume checking for and installing updates." Under the Windows end-user license agreement, users consent to the automatic installation of all updates, features and drivers provided by the service, and to the automatic removal or changes to features being modified is not re**q**uired; it is implicit "without any additional notice".

Redstone 1

Cortana can no longer be fully hidden, as it was made the default search experience in the Windows shell for all users (on previous revisions, a generic search experience without any Cortana branding and functionality is used if it is disabled). As with previous builds, users must still opt-in and grant permission for the software to perform data collection and tracking in order to fully enable Cortana's personalized features. If this functionality is not enabled, Cortana operates in a feature-limited mode with basic web and device search functionality, nearly identical to the non-Cortana search experience on previous builds.

In April 2016, Microsoft announced that it will no longer allow Cortana web searches to be executed through any other web browser and search engine combination but Microsoft Edge and Bing, intentionally disregarding user settings. Microsoft stated that circumvention of these settings (which could be accomplished with third-party software) results in a "compromised experience that is less reliable and predictable", and that only Microsoft Edge supports direct integration with Cortana within the browser itself.

Certain Group Policies no longer have any effect on Windows 10 Home and Pro editions,[134] including disabling Windows Store and Universal Windows Platform apps, "Microsoft consumer experiences" (which pushes tiles to the Start menu for applications not yet installed, such as those placed for apps promoted by Microsoft following a new installation of Windows 10), Windows Tips, turning off the lock screen, or enforcing a specific lock screen background. These changes prevent certain features that have been used for advertising of Windows Store products, such as "Spotlight" tips and app recommendations on the lock screen, from being fully disabled on non-Enterprise editions of Windows 10.

The ability to share Wi-Fi credentials with other contacts via Wi-Fi Sense was removed; Wi-Fi passwords can still be synced between devices tied to the same Microsoft account.

# Chapter 4

## Editions and pricing

Windows 10 editions

Windows 10 is available in four main editions for personal computer devices, of which the Home and Pro versions are sold at retail in most countries, and as pre-loaded software on new computers. Home is aimed at home users, while Pro is aimed at small businesses and enthusiasts. Each edition of Windows 10 includes all of the capabilities and features of the edition below it, and add additional features oriented towards their market segments; for example, Pro adds additional networking and security features such as BitLocker, Device Guard, Windows Update for Business, and the ability to join a domain. The remaining editions, Enterprise and Education, contain additional features aimed towards business environments, and are only available through volume licensing.

As part of Microsoft's unification strategies, Windows products that are based on Windows 10's common platform but meant for specialized platforms are marketed as editions of the operating system, rather than as separate product lines. An updated version of Microsoft's Windows Phone operating system for smartphones, and also tablets, was branded as Windows 10 Mobile.[138] Editions of Enterprise and Mobile will also be produced for embedded systems, along with Windows 10 IoT Core, which is designed specifically for use in small footprint, low-cost devices and Internet of Things (IoT) scenarios and is similar to Windows Embedded.

Preview releases

See also: Windows Insider

A public beta program for Windows 10 known as the Windows Insider Program (previously Windows Technical Preview) began with the first publicly available preview release on October 1, 2014. Insider preview builds are aimed towards enthusiasts and enterprise users for the testing and evaluation of updates and new features. Users of the Windows Insider program receive occasional updates to newer preview builds of the operating system and will continue to be able to evaluate preview releases after general availability (GA) in July 2015— this is in contrast to previous Windows beta programs, where public preview builds were released less frequently and only during the months preceding GA. Windows Insider builds continued being released after the release to manufacturing (RTM) of Windows 10.

Public release

Microsoft promoted that Windows 10 would become generally available (GA) on July 29, 2015. In comparison to previous Windows releases, which had a longer turnover between the release to manufacturing (RTM) and general release to allow for testing by vendors (and in some cases, the development of "upgrade kits" to prepare systems for installation of the new version), an HP Inc. executive explained that because it knew Microsoft targeted the operating system for a release in 2015, the company was able to optimize its then-current and upcoming products for Windows 10 in advance of its release, negating the need for such a milestone.

The general availability build of Windows 10, numbered 10240, was first released on July 15, 2015 to Windows Insider channels for pre-launch testing prior to its formal release. Although a Microsoft official said that there would be no specific RTM build of Windows 10, 10240 was described as an RTM build by media outlets because it was released to all Windows Insider members at once (rather than to users on the "Fast ring" first), it no longer carried pre-release branding and desktop watermark text, and because its build number had mathematical connections to the number 10 in reference to the operating system's naming. The Enterprise edition was released to volume licensing on August 1, 2015.

Users are able to in-place upgrade through the "Get Windows 10" application (GWX) and Windows Update,[155] or the "Media Creation

Tool", which is functionally identical to the Windows 8 online installer, and can also be used to generate an ISO image or USB install media.[156] In-place upgrades are supported from most editions of Windows 7 with Service Pack 1 and Windows 8.1 with Update 1, while users with Windows 8 must first upgrade to Windows 8.1. Changing between architectures (e.g., upgrading from 32-bit edition to a 64-bit editions) via in-place upgrades is not supported; a clean install is required. In-place upgrades may be rolled back to the device's previous version of Windows, provided that 30 days have not passed since installation, and backup files were not removed using Disk Cleanup.

Windows 10 was available in 190 countries and 111 languages upon its launch, and as part of efforts to "re-engage" with users in China, Microsoft also announced that it would partner with Qihoo and Tencent to help promote and distribute Windows 10 in China, and that Chinese PC maker Lenovo would provide assistance at its service centers and retail outlets for helping users upgrade to

Windows 10. At retail, Windows 10 is priced similarly to editions of Windows 8.1, with U.S. prices set at $119 and $199 for Windows 10 Home and Pro respectively. A Windows 10 Pro Pack license allows upgrades from Windows 10 Home to Windows 10 Pro. Retail copies ship on USB flash drive media or DVD-ROM media. New devices shipping with Windows 10 were also released during the operating system's launch window.

Windows RT devices cannot be upgraded to Windows 10.

Free upgrade offer

Windows 10 editions § Free upgrade

During its first year of availability (ended on July 29, 2016),[168] upgrade licenses for Windows 10 could be obtained at no charge for devices with a genuine license for an eligible edition of Windows 7 or 8.1. This offer did not apply to Enterprise editions, as customers under an active Software Assurance (SA) contract with upgrade rights are entitled to obtain

Windows 10 Enterprise under their existing terms. All users running non-genuine copies of Windows, and those without an existing Windows 7 or 8 license, were ineligible for this promotion; although upgrades from a non-genuine version were possible, they result in a non-genuine copy of 10. Microsoft announced in May 2016 that the free upgrade offer would be extended indefinitely to users of assistive technologies; however, Microsoft did not implement any means of certifying eligibility for this offer, which some outlets thereby promoted as being a loophole to fraudulently obtain a free Windows 10 upgrade. Microsoft said that the loophole is not intended to be used in this manner.

On the general availability build of Windows 10, to activate and generate the "digital entitlement" for Windows 10, the operating system must have first been installed as an in-place upgrade. Once installed, the operating system can be reinstalled on that particular system via normal means without a product key, and the system's license will automatically be detected via online activation. As of the November 2015 build, an existing Windows 7 or Windows 8.1 product key can be entered during installation to activate the free license, without the need to upgrade first to "activate" the hardware with Microsoft's activation servers. The Windows Insider Preview version of Windows 10 automatically updated itself to the generally released version as part of the version progression, and continues to be updated to new beta builds, as it had throughout the testing process. Microsoft explicitly stated that Windows Insider was not a valid upgrade path for those running a version of Windows that is ineligible for the upgrade offer; although, if it was not installed with a license carried over from an in-place upgrade to 10 Insider Preview from Windows 7 or 8, the Insider Preview does remain activated as long as the user does not exit the Windows Insider program.


The offer was promoted and delivered via the "Get Windows 10" application ("GWX"), which was automatically installed via Windows Update ahead of Windows 10's release, and activated on systems deemed eligible for the upgrade offer. Via a notification area icon, users could access an application that advertised Windows 10 and the free upgrade offer, check device compatibility, and "reserve" an automatic download of the operating system upon its release. On July 28, a pre-download process began in which Windows 10 installation files were downloaded to some computers that had reserved it. Microsoft said that those who reserved Windows 10 would be able to install it through GWX in a phased rollout process. The operating system could alternatively be downloaded at any time using a separate "Media Creation Tool" setup program (similar to Windows 8's setup program), that allows for the creation of DVD or USB installation media.

Licensing

During upgrades, Windows 10 licenses are not tied directly to a product key. Instead, the license status of the system's current installation of Windows is migrated, and a "Digital entitlement" is generated during the activation process, which is bound to the hardware information collected during the process. If Windows 10 is reinstalled cleanly and there have not been any significant hardware changes since installation (such as a motherboard change), the online activation process will automatically recognize the system's digital entitlement if no product key is entered during installations. However, unique product keys are still distributed within retail copies of Windows 10. As with previous non-volume-licensed versions of Windows, significant hardware changes will invalidate the digital entitlement, and require Windows to be re-activated.

Updates and support

Windows 10 is serviced in a significantly different manner from previous releases of Windows. Its delivery is often described by Microsoft as a "service", due to its ongoing updates, with Terry Myerson explaining that Microsoft's aim is that "the question 'what version of Windows are you running' will cease to make sense."

Unlike previous versions of Windows, Windows Update does not allow the selective installation of updates, and all updates (including patches, feature updates, and driver software) are downloaded and installed automatically. Users can only choose whether their system will reboot automatically to install updates when the system is inactive, or be notified to schedule a reboot. It is possible, however, to defer the download of updates if they are received over a WiFi (not Ethernet) network by marking the WiFi connection as metered (this will also slow program updates, file synchronisation, and live tile updating). Updates can cause compatibility or other problems; a Microsoft troubleshooter program allows bad updates to be uninstalled.

Windows Update can also use a peer to peer system for distributing updates; by default, users' bandwidth is used to distribute previously downloaded updates to other users, in combination with Microsoft servers. Users can instead choose to only use peer-to-peer updates within their local area network.

The original RTM release of Windows 10 ("Windows 10, released in July 2015") receives mainstream support for five years after its original release, followed by five years of extended support, but this is subject to conditions. Microsoft's support lifecycle policy for the operating system notes that "Updates are cumulative, with each update built upon all of the updates that preceded it", that "a device needs to install the latest update to remain supported", and that a device's ability to receive future updates will depend on hardware compatibility, driver availability, and whether the device is within the OEM's "support period"—a new aspect not accounted for in lifecycle policies for previous versions. Microsoft initially said that Windows 10 would freely receive updates for the "supported lifetime of the device." To comply with U.S. accounting laws, revenue for Windows 10 is deferred "on a straight-line basis over the estimated period the software upgrades are expected to be provided by estimated device life", defined as two to four years depending on "customer type."

# Chapter 5

## Upgraded builds

Windows 10 version history

Upgraded builds of Windows 10 will occasionally be released, containing new features and other major improvements. The pace at which upgrades are received is dependent on which release channel is used; the default branch for all users of Windows 10 Home and Pro is "Current Branch", (CB) which receives stable builds as they are publicly released by Microsoft. Windows Insider branches receive unstable builds as they are released, at either a "Fast" pace (immediately after release) or "Slow" pace (slightly delayed from their "Fast" release). The Pro and Enterprise editions may optionally use the "Current Branch for Business" release channel (CBB, referred to in Windows Update settings as "Defer upgrades"), which receives the stable builds on a roughly four-month delay from their CB release.CBB may defer build upgrades for up to eight months, after which the new build must be installed in order to maintain support and access to security updates.Administrators can also use the "Windows Update for Business" service to organize structured deployments of updates and build upgrades across their networks.[186] By installing Windows 10 upgrades, installed programs may be subject to automatic removal if declared "incompatible".

Windows 10 Enterprise can also use the "Long-term support branch" (LTSB). LTSB milestones of Windows 10 are periodic snapshots of Windows 10's CBB branch, and will receive only critical patches over their 10-year support lifecycle. Systems can also be placed one or two versions behind the most recent LTSB build to allow for structured deployments and internal lifecycles. Microsoft director Stella Chernyak explained that "we have businesses [that] may have mission-critical environments where we respect the fact they want to test and stabilize the environment for a long time."

## Threshold 2

The second stable build of Windows 10, build 10586 (also known as the November Update or version 1511, and codenamed "Threshold 2" (TH2)), began to be distributed via Windows Update on November 12, 2015. It contains various improvements to the operating system, its user interface, bundled services, as well as the introduction of Skype-based universal messaging apps, and the Windows Store for Business and Windows Update for Business features.

On November 21, 2015, 10586 was temporarily pulled from public distribution. The upgrade was re-instated on November 24, 2015, with Microsoft stating that the removal was due to a bug that caused privacy and data collection settings to be reset to defaults when installing the upgrade.

## Redstone 1

The third stable build of Windows 10 (officially branded as the Anniversary Update or version 1607, and codenamed "Redstone 1" (RS1)), was released on August 2, 2016, a little over one year after the first stable release of Windows 10. The "Redstone" branch is expected to comprise two major stable builds. While both were originally to be released during 2016, it was later reported that the second had been delayed into 2017 so that it would be released in concert with that year's wave of Microsoft first-party devices.

The Redstone branch introduces new features such as the Windows Ink platform, which eases the ability to add stylus input support to Universal Windows Platform apps and provides a new "Ink Workspace" area with links to pen-oriented apps and features, enhancements to Cortana's proactive functionality, a dark user interface theme mode, a new version of Skype designed to work with the Universal Windows Platform, improvements to Universal Windows Platform intended for video games, and offline scanning using

Windows Defender. Redstone also supports Windows Subsystem for Linux, a new component that provides an environment for running Linux-compatible binary software in an Ubuntu-based user mode environment

On new installations of Windows 10 on systems with secure boot enabled, all kernel mode drivers issued after July 29, 2015 must be digitally signed with an Extended Validation Certificate issued by Microsoft.

Redstone 2

The fourth stable build of Windows 10 (officially branded as the Creator's Update, and codenamed "Redstone 2" (RS2)), was officially announced on October 26, 2016. The branch primarily focuses on content creation, productivity, and gaming features—with a particular focus on virtual and augmented reality (including HoloLens and virtual reality headsets) and on easing the creation of three-dimensional content. It is expected to be released in early-2017.

It introduces a revamped UWP version of Microsoft Paint known as Paint 3D. There will also be a virtual reality workspace designed for use with headsets; Microsoft announced that several OEMs were planning to release VR headsets designed for use with the Creator's Update. Integration with Microsoft acquisition Beam.pro will be added for video game broadcasting on Windows 10 . A new feature known as "My People" will display shortcuts to "important" contacts on the taskbar; notifications involving them will appear above their respective picture, and users can communicate with the contact via either Skype, e-mail, or text messaging (integrating with Android and Windows 10 Mobile devices). Support for additional services, including Xbox, Skype for Business, and third-party integration, will be added in the future. Files can also be dragged directly to the contact's picture to share them.

Future developments

On December 7, 2016, Microsoft announced that as part of a partnership with Qualcomm, it planned to introduce support for running Win32 software on ARM architecture with a 32-bit x86 processor emulator, in 2017. Terry Myerson stated that this move would enable the production of Qualcomm Snapdragon-based Windows devices with cellular connectivity and improved power efficiency over Intel-compatible devices, but are still capable of running the majority of existing Windows software (unlike the previous Windows RT, which was restricted to Windows Store apps). Microsoft is initially targeting this project towards laptops.

System requirements

The basic hardware requirements to install Windows 10 are the same as for Windows 8.1 and Windows 8, and only slightly higher than Windows 7. The 64-bit versions require a CPU that supports certain instructions. Devices with low storage capacity must provide a USB flash drive or SD card with sufficient storage for temporary files during upgrades.

Some pre-built devices may be described as "certified" by Microsoft. Certified tablets must include Power, Volume up, and Volume down keys; ⊞ Win and Rotation lock keys are no longer required.

As with Windows 8, all certified devices must ship with UEFI Secure Boot enabled by default. Unlike Windows 8, OEMs are no longer required to make Secure Boot settings user-configurable, meaning that devices may optionally be locked to run only Microsoft-signed operating systems. A supported infrared-illuminated camera is required for Windows Hello face authentication.[232] Device Guard requires a UEFI system with no third-party certificates loaded, and CPU virtualization extensions (including SLAT and IOMMU) enabled in firmware.

In January 2016, Microsoft announced that Windows 10 will be the only Windows platform that it will officially support on known future CPU microarchitectures; Windows 7 and Windows 8.1 support for systems using Intel's Skylake processors will be phased out; and beginning with the upcoming generations of Intel (Kaby Lake) and AMD

(Bristol Ridge) architectures, Windows 10 will be the only Windows platform supported. Further in the future, using the latest generation processors will always require the latest generation operating system. Terry Myerson said that Microsoft did not want to make further investments in optimizing older versions of Windows and associated software for newer generations of processors.

Reception

TechRadar felt that Windows 10 would be "the new Windows 7", citing the operating system's more familiar user interface, improvements to bundled apps, performance improvements, a "rock solid" search system, and the Settings app being more full-featured than its equivalents on 8 and 8.1. The Microsoft Edge web browser was praised for its performance, albeit not being in a feature-complete state on-launch. While considering them a "great idea in principle", concerns were shown for Microsoft's focus on the universal app ecosystem, noting that "It's by no means certain that developers are going to flock to Windows 10 from iOS and Android simply because they can convert their apps easily. It may well become a no-brainer for them, but at the moment a conscious decision is still required."


Engadget was similarly positive, noting that the upgrade process was painless, and that Windows 10's user interface had balanced aspects of Windows 8 with those of previous versions with a more mature aesthetic. Cortana's always-on voice detection was considered to be its "true strength", also citing its query capabilities and personalization features, but noting that it was not as pre-emptive as Google Now. Windows 10's stock applications were praised for being improved over their Windows 8 counterparts, and for supporting windowed modes. The Xbox app was also praised for its Xbox One streaming functionality, although recommending its use over a wired network due to inconsistent quality over Wi-Fi. In conclusion, it was argued that "Windows 10 delivers the most refined desktop experience ever from Microsoft, and yet it's so much more than that. It's also a decent tablet OS, and it's ready for a world filled with hybrid devices. And, barring another baffling screwup, it looks like a significant step forward for mobile. Heck, it makes the Xbox One a more useful machine."

Ars Technica noted that Windows 10's new Start menu system had an artificial cap of 500 entries, and that any apps beyond this cap would not appear in the Start menu's "All apps" view, nor search results. The new Tablet mode interface was panned for removing the charms and app switching, making the Start button harder to use by requiring users to reach for the button on the bottom-left rather than at the center of the screen when swiping with a thumb, and for making application switching less instantaneous through the use of Task View. Microsoft Edge was praised for being "tremendously promising", and "a much better browser than Internet Explorer ever was", but criticized it for its lack of functionality on-launch. In conclusion, contrasting Windows 8 as being a "reliable" platform albeit consisting of unfinished concepts, Windows 10 was considered "the best Windows yet" and was praised for having a better overall concept in its ability to be "comfortable and effective" across a wide array of form factors, but that it was buggier than previous versions of Windows were on-launch.

ExtremeTech considered that Windows 10 restricted the choices of users, citing its more opaque setting menus, forcing users to give up bandwidth for the peer-to-peer distribution of updates, and for taking away user control of specific functions, such as updates, explaining that "it feels, once again, as if Microsoft has taken the seed of a good idea, like providing users with security updates automatically, and shoved the throttle to maximum." Especially in combination with the free upgrade offer, some outlets also noted that Windows 10 heavily emphasized freemium services, such as media storefronts, Office 365, and paid functionality in bundled games such as Microsoft Solitaire Collection—which requires purchase of a subscription to remove in-game advertising and unlock additional features, even though said features were added to the app's Windows 8 version in March 2013.

## Market share and sales

Twenty-four hours after it was released, Microsoft announced that more than 14 million devices were running Windows 10. On August 26, Microsoft said more than 75 million devices were running Windows 10, in 192 countries, and on more than 90,000 unique PC or tablet models. According to Terry Myerson, there were more than 110 million devices running Windows 10 as of October 6, 2015. On January 4, 2016, Microsoft reported that Windows 10 had been activated on more than 200 million devices since the operating system's launch in July 2015.

In the monthly hardware survey conducted by the video game distribution platform Steam, approximately 34.05% of all devices surveyed ran a version of Windows 10 (either 32-bit or 64-bit architecture) as of January 2016, in comparison to 42.08% using Windows 7.

On 64-bit architecture only, Windows 10 was used by 32.77%, behind 34.31% on Windows 7 64-bit.

According to StatCounter, Windows 10 overtook Windows 8.1 in December 2015.

According to StatCounter market share statistics (based on web use proxy), Iceland was the first country where Windows 10 was ranked first (not only on the desktop, it also holds across all platforms), with several bigger European countries following (a British Crown dependency Isle of Man got there first ahead of any country, late in 2015) and others such as Canada (most popular on desktops; iOS still more popular, ranked first). For one week late in November 2016, Windows 10 overtook first rank from Windows 7 in the United States, before losing it again; it still is more popular every weekend.

At the end of June 2016, Windows 10 had been installed on nearly 350 million devices. By the end of September, this number had become 400 million.

## Update system changes

Windows 10 Home is permanently set to download all updates automatically, including cumulative updates, security patches, and drivers, and users cannot individually select updates to install or not.Microsoft offers a diagnostic tool that can be used to hide updates and prevent them from being reinstalled, but only after they had been already installed, then uninstalled without rebooting the system. Tom Warren of The Verge felt that, given web browsers such as Google Chrome had already adopted such an automatic update system, such a requirement would help to keep all Windows 10 devices secure, and felt that "if you're used to family members calling you for technical support because they've failed to upgrade to the latest Windows service pack or some malware disabled Windows Update then those days will hopefully be over."

Concerns were raised that due to these changes, users would be unable to skip the automatic installation of updates that are faulty or cause issues with certain system configurations—although build upgrades will also be subject to public beta testing via Windows Insider program. There were also concerns that the forced installation of driver updates through Windows Update, where they were previously designated as "optional", could cause conflicts with drivers that were installed independently of Windows Update. An example of such a situation occurred just prior to the general release of the operating system, when an Nvidia graphics card driver that was automatically pushed to Windows 10 users via Windows Update caused issues that prevented the use of certain functions, or prevented their system from booting at all.

Criticism was also directed towards Microsoft's decision to no longer provide specific details on the contents of cumulative updates for Windows 10. On February 9, 2016, Microsoft retracted this decision and began to provide release notes for cumulative updates on the Windows website.

Some users reported that during the installation of the November upgrade, some applications (particularly utility programs such as CPU-Z and Speccy) were automatically uninstalled during the upgrade process, and some default programs were reset to Microsoft-specified defaults (such as Photos app, and Microsoft Edge for PDF viewing), both without warning.

Further issues were discovered upon the launch of the Anniversary Update ("Redstone"), including a bug that caused some devices to freeze (but addressed by cumulative update KB3176938, released on August 31, 2016), and that fundamental changes to how Windows handles webcams had caused many to stop working.

Distribution practices

Microsoft has received mixed reception for its methods of promoting the free upgrade. The main subject of criticism is the "Get Windows 10" (GWX) program used to advertise and initiate the download, which was first downloaded and installed via patch KB3035583 in March 2015 for Windows 8.1; a Computerworld writer felt the program constituted a "nag". Microsoft has also received criticism for using deceptive user interfaces to coax users into installing the operating system, downloading installation files without user consent,[263][262] and making it difficult for users to suppress the advertising and notifications if they do not wish to upgrade to 10. Registry keys and group policies can be used to partially disable the GWX mechanism, but the installation of patches to the GWX software via Windows Update may reset these keys back to defaults, and thus reactivate the software. Third-party programs have also been created to assist users in applying measures to mitigate the GWX mechanism.

In September 2015, it was reported that Microsoft was triggering automatic downloads of the Windows 10 installation files on all compatible Windows 7 or 8.1 computers with Windows Update configured to automatically download and install updates, regardless of whether or not they had specifically requested the upgrade. Microsoft officially confirmed the change, claiming it was "an industry practice that reduces time for installation and ensures device readiness." This move has been criticized by users who have data caps or devices with low storage capacity, as resources were consumed by the automatic downloads of up to 6 GB of data. Other critics argued that Microsoft should not have triggered any downloading of Windows 10 installation files without user consent.

In October 2015, Windows 10 began to appear as an "Optional" update in the Windows Update interface, but checked off for installation on some systems. A Microsoft spokesperson said that this was a mistake, and that the download would no longer be checked off by default.[14] However, on October 29, 2015, Microsoft announced that it planned to consider Windows 10 as a "recommended" update in the Windows Update interface some time in 2016, which will cause an automatic download of installation files and a one-time prompt with a choice to install to appear. In December 2015, it was reported that a new advertising dialog had begun to appear, only containing "Upgrade now" and "Upgrade tonight" buttons, and no obvious method to decline installation besides the close button.

In March 2016, some users also alleged that their Windows 7 and 8.1 devices had automatically begun upgrading to 10 without their consent. In June 2016, the GWX dialog's behavior changed to make closing the window imply a consent to a scheduled upgrade. Despite this, an Infoworld editor disputed the claims that upgrades had begun without any consent at all; testing showed that the upgrade to Windows 10 would only begin once the user accepts the end-user license agreement (EULA) presented by its installer, and that not doing so would eventually cause Windows Update to time out with an error, thus halting the installation attempt. It was concluded that these users may have unknowingly clicked the "Accept" prompt without full knowledge that this would begin the upgrade.


On January 21, 2016, Microsoft was sued in small claims court by a user whose computer, shortly after the release of the OS, had attempted to upgrade to Windows 10 without her consent. The upgrade failed, and her computer was left in an unstable state thereafter, which disrupted the ability to run her travel agency. The court ruled in favor of the user and awarded her $10,000 in damages, but Microsoft appealed. However, in May 2016, Microsoft dropped the appeal and chose to pay the damages. Shortly after the suit was reported on by the Seattle Times, Microsoft confirmed that it was updating the GWX software once again to add more explicit options for opting out of a free Windows 10 upgrade; the new notification is a full-screen pop-up window notifying users of the impending end of the free upgrade offer, and contains "Remind me later", "Do not notify me again" and "Notify me three more times" options.

Privacy and data collection

Privacy advocates and other critics have expressed concern regarding Windows 10's privacy policies and its collection and use of customer data. Under the default "Express" settings, Windows 10 is configured to send various information to Microsoft and other parties, including the collection of user contacts, calendar data, and "associated input data" to personalize "speech, typing, and inking input", typing and inking data to improve recognition, allowing apps to use a unique "advertising ID" for analytics and advertising personalization (functionality introduced by Windows 8.1) and allow apps to request the user's location data and send this data to Microsoft and "trusted partners" to improve location detection (Windows 8 had similar settings, except that location data collection did not include "trusted partners"). Users can opt out from most of this data collection, but telemetry data for error reporting and usage is also sent to Microsoft, and this cannot be disabled on non-Enterprise versions of Windows 10. Microsoft's privacy policy states, however, that "Basic"-level telemetry data is anonymized and cannot be used to identify an individual user or device. The use of Cortana also requires the collection of data "such as your device location, data from your calendar, the apps you use, data from your emails and text messages, who you call, your contacts and how often you interact with them on your device" to personalize its functionality.

Rock Paper Shotgun writer Alec Meer argued that Microsoft's intent for this data collection lacked transparency, stating that "there is no world in which 45 pages of policy documents and opt-out settings split across 13 different settings screens and an external website constitutes 'real transparency'." ExtremeTech pointed out that, while previously scroogling against Google for similar data collection strategies, "[Microsoft] now hoovers up your data in ways that would make Google jealous." However, it was also pointed out that the requirement for such vast usage of customer data had become a norm, citing the increased reliance on cloud computing and other forms of external processing, as well as similar data collection requirements for services on mobile devices such as Google Now and Siri. In August 2015, Russian politician Nikolai Levichev called for Windows 10 to be banned from use within the Russian government, as it sends user data to servers in the United States. The country had passed a federal law requiring all online services to store the data of Russian users on servers within the country by September 2016, or be blocked. Writing for ZDNet, Ed Bott said that the lack of complaints by businesses about privacy in Windows 10 indicated "how utterly normal those privacy terms are in 2015." In a Computerworld editorial, Preston Gralla said, "The kind of information Windows 10 gathers is no different from what other operating systems gather. But Microsoft is held to a different standard than other companies."

Microsoft Services Agreement reads that the company's online services may automatically "download software updates or configuration changes, including those that prevent you from accessing the Services, playing counterfeit games, or using unauthorized hardware peripheral devices." Critics interpreted this statement as implying that Microsoft would scan for and delete unlicensed software installed on devices running Windows 10. However, others pointed out that this agreement was specifically for Microsoft online services such as Microsoft account, Office 365, Skype, as well as Xbox Live, and that the offending passage most likely referred to digital rights management on Xbox consoles and first-party games, and not plans to police pirated video games installed on Windows 10 PCs. Despite this, some torrent trackers announced plans to block Windows 10 users, also arguing that the operating system could send information to anti-piracy groups that are affiliated with Microsoft. Writing about these allegations, Ed Bott of ZDNet compared Microsoft's privacy policy to Apple's and Google's and concluded that "after carefully reading the Microsoft Services Agreement, the Windows license agreement...and the Microsoft Privacy Statement carefully, I don't see anything that looks remotely like Big Brother." Columnist Kim Komando argued that "Microsoft might in the future run scans and disable software or hardware it sees as a security threat," consistent with the Windows 10 update policy.

# Conclusion

Thank you again for downloading this book!

I hope this book was able to help you to UNDERSTAND the basic steps of WINDOW 10.

Finally, if you enjoyed this book, then I'd like to ask you for a favor, would you be kind enough to leave a review for this book on Amazon? It'd be greatly appreciated!

Thank you and good luck!

I truly do appreciate it!

Best Wishes,

Lee Maxwell

www.ingramcontent.com/pod-product-compliance
Lightning Source LLC
Chambersburg PA
CBHW061028050326

40689CB00012B/2736